MAR — 5 2008

CROSSING THE GREAT DIVIDE

Poems
by
Jean Feraca

D1566606

Printed in the United States of America.
Designed by University Publications, Madison, Wisconsin.

Front cover photographs:
The two towns of Grisolia and Maiera facing each other across a
deep crevice overlooking the Mediterranean, from *Italian Hilltowns*,
published by Documan Press, Kalamazoo, Michigan, copyright
© 1979. Used by permission.
The poet's maternal grandmother, Vincenza ("Jenny")
Zetena Sinisgalli.

Cover design by Barry Carlsen, University Publications Office,
University of Wisconsin–Madison..

ISBN 1-882280-008 (pbk.) $9.95

This book is dedicated to Felix Pollak
who "whenever I settled back . . .
started in again, nag, nag, nag,
'du musst dein Leben äendern'. . .
in the voice of an uncle"
—even after death.

The life that held too tight escapes
Will ever after run
With a prudential look behind
And specters of the rein.

Emily Dickinson

Acknowledgements

Grateful acknowledgement is made to the editors and the publishers of the following anthologies and periodicals in which these poems were first published, sometimes in different versions or with different titles:

Adena, "Bedouin," "Nadia in Black Among the Cuttlefish"
American Poetry Review, "Backstairs," "Botanical Gardens"
Anon, "January Thaw"
Calapooya Collage, "Grace Notes"
The Dream Book, "Nursing My Child Through His First Illness,"
    "Scirocco," "Vision in the Grove"
Festival of Poets, "Pond God"
Green House, "Nadia's Breasts," "Nursing My Child Through His
    First Illness"
The Green River Review, "Troubled Sleep"
The Iowa Review, "Waking Early After Heavy Snow"
Isthmus, "Nadia in Black Among the Cuttlefish"
Kentucky Renaissance, "Elegy for Jenny," "Heart Attack," "Snow
    Flurries," "Waking Early After Heavy Snow"
La Poesia Femminista, "Elegy for Jenny"
The Nation, "Caves," "Heart Attack," "Elegy for Jenny," "Erice,"
    "South Paradise Hotel"
The Southern Review, "January Thaw," "Snow Flurries"
The Transylvanian, "All These Months," "La Bini"
Two Decades of New Poets, "Botanical Gardens"
Wisconsin Poetry, "Botanical Gardens," "Of Bread"
Wisconsin Poets' Calendar 1988, "Of Bread"

Dedication derived from *Benefits of Doubt*, by Felix Pollak, published by Spoon River Poetry Press, 1988.

Emily Dickinson excerpt borrowed from *The Complete Poems of Emily Dickinson*, edited by Thomas H. Johnson, published by Little, Brown and Company, 1960.

The poems collected in Part I of this book, "Traveling South From Rome," first appeared in *South From Rome: Il Mezzogiorno*, published in a limited edition by Larkspur Press, Monterey, Kentucky, 1976, with assistance of a grant from the National Endowment for the Arts.

The lines, "I am looking for you. I find you in the next seat./ Your shoulder is against mine," from "Convalescing in the East Sisters' Weavers' House," are adapted from Poem #25 of *The Kabir Book*, translated by Robert Bly.

In addition, I wish to thank Grace Schulman for her abiding inspiration and support; Donald Hall, who taught me how to write poetry; Andrea Potos, without whose interest and encouragement this book would not have been possible; Susan Elbe, who served as editor; and the Wisconsin Arts Board, for its generous support which made possible the completion of this manuscript.

Table of Contents

PART III: SAILING TO AMERICA

Part I

Traveling South From Rome

Erice

Your hair is soft
white as dead grass
whispering, full of the eyes of old women.

Full of sighs
and hissing, the sea of your voice, its long
skinny arms
pleading with the sand, the tiny shells.

You wait by the church doors, all fringe
and rags, your hands are beggars
they cry from the steps
as I pass.

2

Left
like treasure on a mountain, a dagger
honed in wind
high above the plain, you
tilt, as

one
by one, the clouds
rise from the sea
and cross
over Trapani . . .

(the wind flicks a tongue in the eucalyptus
incestuous
incestuous
the fan palm glitters on the hill)

Hooded mummer, wound
in fog
clasped like a lover in his secret flesh

slowly your mind
spins
out of the gray rock
I follow you through a maze . . .
you draw me like the thought of my own death.

3

Cold, the streets at dawn slink like cats
and disappear. Mists
in the piazza
swirl like drowning sails
and the same
lame dog
keeps passing, its nails
click like teeth over the slick
wet stone.

In Catania

This must be the baron's chamber
under the crest
the cracked
moulding
the lace feet of mice
I dream while the carpets ravel

It's raining in this room
How long have the walls been so helpless?
the arms
of the rain so long, so yellow?
I reach toward the light, the

glass chandelier swimming from its chain
above the bed . . .

Down here in this crypt, the mind
cracks
like a safe.
I'm the black-gloved thief with a gunnysack.
I'm the bishop, stripped.

Entrails hang in the market, yellow jackets
fastened
in the livers of sheep.
This drilling in the mind goes on, incessant.
How long, this butcher's hand, this probe for eggs?

You're all the way up in the dark on the landing.
You roll with the dust. Lace
curtains flap. How do I bat my way up
through this hive, this
buzzing in my head, this
storm of feathers breaking up like quarry rock?

Three Sisters

Maria

What dark self is this heaped behind a counter
at the House of Berlitz?
Behind each lens, the eyes swim up, dim fish.
Thick as a mist, she rises from her desk.
Who could love that flatboned face, naked as a tooth?
That pallid skin bruised mushroom-brown.
Sister Scribe, head stuffed in your chest,
you breathe in loam
domed over cramped space
like a toad in a cellar well.

Valentina

Cancelled. Stamped flat as ink in your rumpled smock.
Behind that grid, I recognize myself. Those lidded eyes
pulled taut as sheets give back my own.
A postal clerk, you live alone. Your pain yanked to the
        top of your head,
you're wired, every line alive, shot through with hate.
You crackle at the mouth, twitch on and off like neon in the cheek.
Sister Spinster, you deal your stamps across the space,
your hands stained yellow at the nail,
betrayed, betrayed, betrayed
by nicotine, chipped dark red paint.

Bloodsisters,

What was it we buried together and forgot
so long ago?
When we pricked each other's thumbs and mixed
        the blood,
what was lost under that oak?
a photograph? a map? a key?

We're all come home, small round stones
a circle of laps. Come, take hands.
This our pact: we three one
claim each other kin,
Sister Worm, Mother Mole, Sister Sin.

Cat Lady in the Villa Borghese

Bunched, misery-linked, they sit together on a green bench:
A hag and two cats. Each back carries its hump.
The cats doze after the feast.
She reads her paper through a glass
pouch-eyed walnut face soaking in the sun.
At last she sighs, scatters the cats like crumbs.

She drags the gravel paths between the curbs
umbrella trailing in the dust, past the summerhouse
and the swans, indifferent as a blight.
Past Venus, babies, newlyweds, Savonarola and the stone boar.
She picks the garden like a scab.

Between the black, rain-streaked acacia trunks she moves
in her flame-blue scarf, steady as a shuttle
through a loom, weaving sun to shade,
and the sack she carries
swells by her side;
I follow her everywhere, gathering all afternoon.

She works until the sun snags in a far hedge.
Lovers thin, the whir of doves;
The park grows dank.
Inside the walls, she pauses under sweet Lorenzo's
stone-eyed gaze to count her take.
Then I lose her in the crowd disappearing through an iron gate.

Vision in the Grove

*". . . and this is the sixth month
with her that is called barren."*

1

Driving to Roccella Ionica, east across the boot
through a forest of hair
rank
as pubic growth. Prickly-pear
erupts in the rockwall, a cancer of thumbs.
Lizards clash, geranium jetting over the edge like blood.

Suddenly I am sick of it: this harsh landscape
running to extremes
the south, the struggle to survive—
Agave with its horn
thrusts
its way out of my side;
honey-coy, the locust hides its thorn.

Let me unlearn these hills
I have loved,
scogliera needling the shore; my ancestors
saracen-faced, your speech thick as the black wine
you swill, eyes brooding under cliffs.
I carry the itch of those looks
under my skin for days.

It's april in the North Atlantic States, the maples
pushing out their sticky leaves like scouts.
Here, the honeysuckle already brown
the mouth of the rose
blown wide,
it hurts. I close my eyes
dream my way back to olive groves
we passed at dawn:

Goia Tauro, Laureana, Taureanova
old hags, old crones,
I call you like a congress of great aunts
your crooked trunks unhook
a universe of moss
and rime
that drifts, a sinewy smoke. Your wrinkled
rippling flanks unleash black rain
to nets below. You grow like scars
beyond yourselves you dream
you're young again, wandering the grove
loose as snakes
weaving each other's necks and waists.

Lulled by the haze, I stay
a long time.
The grove fills. Calves brushed
by dew, I move through dawn-soft air,
wet light mewing in the leaves
I pick my steps
with care, until my walk
becomes a kind of swim
through long wet grass
I am drenched
newborn
swimming in a sea without a name.

Post-Partum

for Giancarlo

Stunned, like a fish by a blow
I lie in the green
near bottom
spinning a fin
belly lolling toward the sun

far, far above, you flit through the cage
of weeds
that was your mother, your swamp

we've changed places, you and I
you took the air
bursting into light like a swallow from a barn
now it is I who thrash and thump about down here in the blood-
blind clubfoot dark

your hands wave above the crib, white moths
fanning back the dark . . .

oh my berry, my sweet black frog, we are lost
holding each other's trembling
like an old man's hands

Nursing My Child through His First Illness

Lucania, 1974

1

Sleepless he rages, fists on the rails
howling for hours . . .

This, the old dream to be martyred
the calling denied
floats up, a kidney in a bowl
carried to the altar, St. Agatha's breasts
Ophelia's face

the procession of virgins advances, she carries
a candle
she wears a white dress

a thimble rolls out of my grandmother's coffin
I am bound on the hoop sewn into my hem

This is the way, each moment
I mount
ever higher, the life
of the flesh
falls away

knock knock knock

upstairs, the invalid thumps with his cane
from the bed

knock knock knock

in his three-legged
crib, the infant stands up.

2

I live alone on the edge of town
I keep my father's house

Remember, O most gracious virgin mary
never was it known that anyone who fled
to thy protection
was left
unaided . . .

Skull-bald, these mountains hang over us
massive and terrible
leaning like great-aunts over an infant's cradle.

3

teeth descend from the cave roof in rows
Mouth
under the Mountain

O mother of the word incarnate
before thee I stand
sinful and sorrowful

a tower extrudes from a hill
salt
laps at the edge, uneasy

my darling, I'll croon to you, I'll coo
I'll carry you for hours
your wails
splash my sides like a tide of acid
you wear me away all white

the sea sucks up, shudders
subsides to a hiss
starfish slide
dead crabs float
belly up
the moon spins upside down
I'll croon, I'll coo, I'll carry you for hours

all the rock pools give up their ghosts
in the sun
white algae heaps up in pockets
airy
weightless
I drift, I rove, I carry you for hours

O Mountain, O Rose, O Gold

knock knock knock

pocked, pitted, this blister of rock

white algae heaps up in pockets
despise not my petition
hear me, O Mother
Answer.

La Bini

You might as well be Venus
poised there
thigh-deep in the Mediterranean,
O Transparent Lady, in your white bikini
you're wet as a shell, all sheen and silk!
You dabble your fingertips in limpid
blue, spilling the
iridescent oils of your voice, your laughter rippling.
Each morning you cast your pearls
inquiring after my son
his fever, the color of his spots. What fond
solicitude, nurtured like your milk-fed skin!
I imagine you stepping daintily into the squalor of my hut.
You paint your toenails purple (*"che bello smalto!"*)
while you consort lounges, naked on the terrace.
Careless as an heir apparent, he's fondling
his tiny
terra cotta pipe; fumes rise sleepily
along a wicker stem, curling to the eyes
half-slits. He speaks of Marx
and revolution,
butter rolls around his tongue.
Tonight he'll feed you baby meatballs
in four kinds of cream,
artichokes
sliced with a half-moon knife.

Your sister arrives from the south,
Donatella, a tousled blond, her skin smoldering.
She's taken a panther for a lover.
Look where he sits, crouched there on the ledge,
his long teeth shine. His eyes charge
with fires shepherds set on the mountain.
He's dreaming of Sicilian beaches, the spangled sky,
the cold white scar
slicing its silver through the plush
pathless black of her breast.

Nadia's Breasts

You gypsy boys I glimpse through threadbare blue,
brazen imps, you swing through traffic
dodging whistles, catcalls, hairy-fisted cops
street-smart little hustlers dangling
from the backs of streetcars
you ride the bluish dust
bareass as sparks buzz and snap
hanging by a grin through the clang, the din
the furious horns of Naples!

South Paradise Hotel

It rains every day and we're the only guests.
I listen to your footsteps ring
climbing the terrazzo stair.

You burst in, the geranium explodes.

You carried it all the way from the front yard
cradled under your coat.

This morning in the butcher's shop
I watched with the same
cold eyes
blood spatter the floor.

Scirocco

At noon, bells crack the air. I climb
into light
clattering on the rooftiles.
Above the slamming of shopfronts, wet sheets
slap like sails. The smell of fishhead,
flower-stem, sweeps up in gusts.
In this dirty wind, I hold
a steady watch
wary as a whore in steerage, traveling alone.

Bedouin

She climbed the far side of the dune,
a dot
above a curving line. Then
sudden as a shout she came running, the
small breath rattling like seeds in her lungs.
She held a doll in the car window,
a clutch of shreds begged
from her mother: coconut-hard breasts,
a bit of tin, a red
bandana. But my mind stopped at the face—
a featureless white patch she held
against the eyeless
Sahara—I watched it fade
drop back
empty
into Allah.

Nadia in Black among the Cuttlefish

picks her way through bones
nosed in sand as if they skidded into death;
high up where beachgrass flicks
the wind spits salt
her hands fly up, she calls
headed toward that spur
where gulls
converge

"Gabbiani, gabbiani!"

Just so
the heart beats up
clamorous, summoning its several parts
that flock until the whole
lifts off
throws its reins like a rider lost
far out on the sea's neck,
risks all.

Crossing the Great Divide

Your real country is where you're heading,
not where you are.
        —Rumi

1

Hooked in this space between sea and sky
like a hammock
pitched from a cliff
I stare out at the day, death in the corners of its eyes.

Only the goat-hoofed, the cloven
survive in this place
scrambling for toeholds, hanging in the crags.

The gecko clings with tacky feet to the stucco wall.
Stupefied at noon,
he curves around a roofbeam
abandoning his long body to its love for the hot dark.

I let myself down, inch by inch.
On the ledge, white wine withers in the glass.
I live in the holes.

Life slows to a lizard's pulse,
a hot stone,
I hold the quick between my thumbs, stroking its throat.

2

The sea asleep, brassy serpent
sullen in the shallows now
a muddy swell
slithering through trees below.

I shall live out my life rejoicing
ribboning under the jagged shadow of the hawk.

There is no reason for this joy
eagle-bald, knifing through me like a canyon.

There is nothing in this landscape that defines me.

3

Freed from the past with its priest's hands
we are grails
crossing a great divide,
below us, the abyss, ahead, the dense glass—
Believing we will crash, we are passed
whole
through the rose
the blue
the needle's eye of God.

—Maratea, Lucania

Part II

Caves

Heart Attack

You greet me from the sunken box
of the old chair. Arms
slack on the cracked leather.
Rags of your face strung on lines,
drying. Owls
in round caves of your eyes.

Father, I know you: You dream,
staring into a ditch that
fills with mud and slow water,
your trousers dangle,
shredded from the waist, the pockets
slashed, the money gone.

I want to bite my hands and tear
my cheeks,
to be fifteen and lie facedown
in the darkest corner of my room,
shuddering at every thud
below of oak

chairs knocked to their knees, flung
against the wall.
I want you back again, tyrant.
I want to watch you foam again
in the climb up the hard tide
that all but killed us both.

January Thaw

These days hang
like gray socks filling up
with snow. I am
empty inside them, hollow
as the small caves
of boots
left side by side
to stiffen in the hall.

This is the month
of mud and rain-soaked stumps.
Knucklebones, thin fingers
of snow litter the yard.
A trail of chicken's feet,
fishheads, rinds
and oyster shells leads down
to the ravine. Snow
sticks in shadow
like a corpse of rags.

In the bottom of the night
my grandmother inhabits
the body of a hound. Long
tongues of hair leap and
twist in the air around her face.
In my arms she rolls wild eyes,
howls, drools, whimpers
once, and dies.

Elegy for Jenny

She took a long time to grow old,
moving steadily inward
like an apple abandoning its skin
until she touched
hard seeds at the core.

Long after, hooked at the back
of the open door
her cane knocked softly—

She stood in shadow under the arch
holding up the dim
lamp of her face, white hair rolled
back, cheekbones
almost free. Old
crow in a tree
of ribs, she preached
from the scaffolding of her own bones.

She wandered at the end,
groping in her nightgown down long
halls. They found her
slumped in the Empire chair
white among the shadows
slanting in that room full of thrones.

Caves

I watch you harden
slowly
to stone, tied in your armchair.

Your eyes
are hollows in a wall.

I want to live inside you, the way
darkness lives
crouched
at the bottom of a lake.

When you hunt for yourself
in caves
I want to be darkness
hanging upside down inside you.

I want to suck light from your bones.
When you look for your face
I want to be your reflection.

All These Months

All these months, on my hands and knees
I've pushed you down
like the bulbs I buried in the mud
last spring, the ones
I still wait for.

The memory of you drags at my belly
like a child.

I am afraid. I fear the cat
dead in the ravine,
the owl that watched me in my sleep
last night. I shun you
as I shun priests
sorcerers, and abandoned houses.

The sky moves through the eyebone
of the empty house. All day
I circle you, I walk around
and around, held
like a dancer to a sacrificial pole.

You never came. Outside, the garden
drifts like a spider through a thin backyard.
Thistles ravel in the hedge. My eyes
loop like threads
spinning through wind and sun.

Snow Flurries

Catching sight of you
reading in the half-light of windows
filled with huge, torn flakes
of snow, I love you again
remembering how I found you
ahead in the woods
last summer, unaware of the flurry
of moths
battering behind your head
like a snowball opening
just
short of the mark.

Waking Early After Heavy Snow

While we slept, the snow
fell and pinned us to the bed, sealing
our eyes
shut, filling up
the dreaming holes of our mouths.

Waking numb, we find our bodies
tangled
like wet rope, dense
as bushes deep in the ravine,
each twig
thick as a thumb.

We wait. Slugs of light
slide through the venetian blind,
assemble slowly
on the rug, lengthen, grow fat.

At last we stagger, tug up the window
lids, letting in the white
eyes of day. The woods
sway and start to fall apart, piece
by white piece.

We fumble with spoons, bowls, eggs
and struggle, like those crocuses
that let their saw-teeth part
too soon, and have to fight
all day to hold up
heavy yellow cups half-filled with snow.

Backstairs

Damp air clinging with its sticky mouths
to my skin, I move uneasily
through the night. Intense
insect eyes
spy from the unmown grass,
greedy as thieves
or lovers. Suddenly
I understand why you hated
me, glued like a snail
to the window on the backstairs
feeding in secret, eating you with my eyes.

Pond God

He is the Bog's dark father.
Uncle of leeches, eels and polliwogs
he keeps the lily pads afloat
the lilies in their cups,
he lets the clams conspire.
Because of him, the green heron lifts its bill,
cypress dribble leafhair, roots,
worms push through moss.
He makes the sand turn gold and ripple into ribs.
He makes the mud bloom.
Ruling over reeds and mare's tail,
all things in his sway
he pumps like a bullfrog from his throne:
Kingfisher, dragonfly,
even minnows who slip through their quicksilver schools
rise from his rich, black heart.

Botanical Gardens

Beyond the steaming glass and the massed
leaves, alone
in the sunken room, I am serene.
Orchids sway toward me out of the Chinese vases
and here above the blue
seas of the carpet, I still sail
in your wake; I close my eyes and find
the whole garden floating up, an island
rising inside me.

Each time I find you, all the sorrows
rush out of me like rain
from wet pine. I feel huge
and light, like the elm balancing
on one leg, dancing
like Shiva—
all her great ecstatic arms wheeling and furling
in the air, obedient to each impulse,
at home with desire.

Part III

Sailing to America

Sailing to America

Why have I called you 'Mother'
in my sleep?
　　　　—Robin Morgan

In the bath, you stroke my breasts
furrowing the mounds where sparrows nest
you blaze a set of tracks
through wave on wave of prairie grass
brush forth, back
back, forth—
my breasts
turn into boys on board a ship
emigrants, each with a cap.
Together by the rail we stand transfixed
sure of nothing but this steady tow
that laps, laps
sucking at our sides—
Someone who loved us once is calling, calling
like a mother from another life—
we ride each wave, whitecaps crest
foam up like cream,
O what a rich ocean this is! Her voice
tilts us to the wind, curls our sails crisp
calling, calling, pulling us
until it stops.
We find ourselves offshore
craning for a view: it lies before us—
America
two leagues off.

Grace Notes

1

I always thought I wanted slender men
sleek as skinned rabbits
But you! Your legs thick hickory
your chest shagbark
I rub against until I come
falling out of your arms like a bird.

———————

2

nimble, fleet, your hands are braves
they climb a ladder home
across a cliff, each toe and handhold warm
following a path that zigzags down
to a ledge between two lips
hidden pueblo, secret
slit

———————

3

In the grotto, pebbles
you fondle
grow wet, little rocks you make gush.
Someone is kneeling, like Bernadette.

———————

4

At the lip of a ledge
you lay your hand, a trickle appears
a rivulet. Petals plunge, rooted in the wet.
Snow seeps black, swelling a stream to foam.
Then headlong down the mountainside, the cataract
comes crashing, bride white.

———————

5

you touch my thighs
they bloom
     azalea
         zinnea
    wild phlox
a wall of fire set in great clay pots
         against the house
    inside
the housewife rests
against a cool, white wall
her breath drawn up in bucketfuls
       spilling out
          dark
      from the well's depths

———————

6

plucked from sleep, I thrash
a fish caught in your net, flash red
white, wheeling for another element
your tongue triggering, arcing me free
hauled into air, my fins sprout wings
filling with wind like flutes
my bones trill for joy.

———————

7

Oh, I am many-layered
multiple
as moons radiating rings, as white
and smooth-skinned as a lake
smelling of mushroom
all my gills ruffling, rippling out . . .

———————

8

Your mouth nibbling the line
a sudden swoop
I climb the sky, your kite.

Of Bread

It doesn't matter that the house isn't locked.
Without you, it's empty as an oven
of its loaves

I want neither your ham nor your cheese
nor your oysters and white
wine

I want the yeast of you, making me rise
til I split, two halves
in your teeth

and the butter melting, the hot bran
your yam-yellow light spilling
your honey seeping all through the comb

Not this house with its darkening oak.
Not that table laid with its cold
plates.

Sagittarius

I take you in (O happy dagger!)
Gorge on you, motherhoard
My plunder

There is no bottom to this well
No quelling
This huge hunger

I thought you were the sea swelling
I thought I was Aphrodite rising from your foam
Who is this monster rides you flat out, flailing

Knees, thighs
Dug in
Goading your thunder?

This must be the underworld we forge
Your colossal legs floundering
Through ungulate water, the air

Roaring, we sink
Into a stew
Thick as sulphur we are galloping through

Brays, bellows, a hullabaloo
Erupts
From the inside—It's bedlam

I'm queen of, rampant
Bared
I snort, shudder

Boil up like a brew, a screamer
Pluming over. Arched
Taut

Ready to leap
Out of time
To be

Released, the flint that flies
One-eyed
Into dawn.

The Zealot

Everything was wet. The pitcher sweated.
Wooden doors swelled up like thumbs.
Saliva pooled from the tongues of the cats.
Even the beeswax candles melted
and keeled over. Only he
stayed dry as a snake, his neck blackening all summer.

I spent whole days comatose, feet propped over the bed
imagining cool layers of white plaster under the white wall.
Mornings I'd wake to the empty rooms and find him
crouched over pots and jars, mixing potions in the garden.
I'd watch his fingers flick and dart among the slick leaves
prying squash blossoms open, shaking out pollen.

Water trickled through the beds. The sky often rippled
and cracked open as I lay among the sheets.
He glided through the heat like an Ethiopian.
Oblivious to all rumblings, he went on tying up tomatoes
until they tottered seven feet over that rank, slippery acre.

The garden festered by caprice, overspreading strings,
trellises he set like traps, violating shapes
he teased and fretted. The pitch of the katydids
rose to a scream as warnings came crackling over the radio.

Screwball! the neighbors taunted, but joined him
with smudge pots, tattered blankets and torches.
Yelling all night through teeth clenched like klansmen
they staved off the inevitable.
Then, it was hopeless.

Rummaging one afternoon, obsessed with loss, his eyes lit
on the zinc trough in the basement. He hauled it up
two floors, rigging ropes and pulleys, hoisting
pebbles by the bucketful. I cringed
as each bucket swung through the window like a wrecker's ball.
He carried in the plants themselves at last
crowing over his plot to outwit nature.

All that winter on the pea-green porch, peppers and tomatoes
sickened and wasted. Flesh molded to vine.
Drooping, fuzzy at first, the coils and goosenecks stiffened.
Each softening cheek stretched to a leathery hide.
Tendrils grew into horns and talons.
They oozed, dripped, gave off fetid vapors.

He never let anything die.

Troubled Sleep

Nightmare fumes around my face like camphor in a sac.
Your shoes are open graves I stumble on.
Your socks, dead birds to gather up.

This is the bottleneck. With every breath
I draw, the rings
constrict. Beside me in the bed
you're like a third rail, rigid with current.

I listen to your mutterings, sort through gibberish
for signs. You thrash, cry out, wrestle with the sheet.
Underneath the El, the house shakes . . .

        I dream my mother's dream
from my grandmother's bed: the eels are all
escaping from the kitchen sink . . .

A blue volt wracks the sky
arcing you awake. Our eyes meet.
The light fails. We plunge through tunnels
pitched headlong. Brakes squeal like pigs.

Fossil

With you, I've lived a million years
waiting
to be flesh again.

Tarantella

I draw the bolt, you jimmy the lock
I yank the shades, you tap at the glass
I'm shut against you like a fort

but you seep through, your foot-
prints multiplying overnight
spreading over the carpet like a dew

Devouring mist
you're in the air I breathe
you're growing in my left breast

I hack you out, but you grow back
hang on, jaws locked
you flop at my back, at my chest

Overhead, your yellow eye
roving like a hawk
you swoop across my yard, your shadow

blowing toward me in my sleep
you're piling high against the door
you're howling like a jackal on the other side

a whiff of me bristles your hock
you sniff the air and bay
begin your long relentless trek

loping out of the desert half-lame
starving, stung by God
raving like a locust plague

you pitch a tent on the edge of town
preaching misery and doom
Jeremiah

I'm the moon
you're the ash on my face
Come, storm me, swarm my gate

I'll pitch you over the top
even if you crack me like a cottonwood
my sap will hiss and issue forth alive

fresh, seething
thriving on your filth
I smear myself with you until I stink.

Beat the tambourine, pour out the wine!
This time, for the sheer joy, for the itch
in the soles of our feet

we dance, we celebrate, we lock once more
our feet begin their wedding jig
our legs and bellies shake

the scorpion flicks its tail erect
as flames close in
your hot breath sweeps my cheek

I'm ready now.
I feel the venom rise.

Sun City

She bakes ceramic frogs.
He joins the Critical Issues Club.

Mornings, thick with phenobarb, he pads into the kitchen,
his old-dog eyes blear with cataract peer up
at the clock. Six a.m. Outside, Dell Web's white wall

flares with its inch of sun. In the silence
he sits. His teeth crunch, grinding oats like a horse.
She comes in.

They've kept it all intact:
his teeth, her breath
the bickering that foams between them like a bromide.

He slips out through the glass doors, still in his robe
at ten, his gnarled legs slither up a ladder,
scattering lizards at the ledge.

For an hour, he waters the roof.
She mops the patio.
The desert is dusty, she sighs, sweeping a sill.

Inside, the house goes on ticking to itself, scentless
as a vault. Twin urns on the mantle, still
precisely cobalt.

At night, the old walnut bed will creak like a boat.
She'll wait until he snores
before sneaking out to crack the window.

She has to breathe *real air,* she says.
She's hoping for some deliverance from this desert.
Something more than what rolls in over the white wall:

Tumbleweed, the smell
of cattle dung. And now, again, that terrible howl
just entering her middle ear as she drops off.

Thallasemia Minor*

1

They come on strong, my poor hemoglobin, racing red
against time, cells teeming through the bloodstream,
thronging gates, threatening gangways like a thrombosis.
Always too many, always too small, following

the message the brain whispers in the marrow, the same
message the priest whispered in the village confessional,
"Fate figli!" "Fate figli!" Breed! Breed! Increase!
They issue forth: Annunziata, Vincenzina, Addolorata . . .

These are your poor, your refuse from a teeming shore.
This, the waste of the last generation to wash over Ellis,
each lumpish hopeful doomed to push until the murmur
in the heart starts up like gossip at the back of the church.

The doctors make inquiries into my ancestry.

2

I think of my grandmother, that Amazon, "Diavola Femmina."
She who threw Casey Stengel down an excavation ditch
as a girl, but kept her "Sonny" at home, that great man
forever plied with duck livers, stuffed capon breast.

---

* Thallasemia minor is a form of inherited anemia found in many
Mediterraneans and southern Chinese. The red blood count is ele-
vated; cells are abnormally small, short-lived and can be cigar-shaped
or otherwise irregular. The condition is benign but carries serious
genetic implications. Thallasemia major is fatal.

Uncles on my father's side: Sal, the eldest, a Mama's boy
wrapped in fedora and black overcoat even in July,
bundled into a beach chair that summer in Far Rockaway.
A doctor, he died of an overdose, facedown in the street.

Then came James, the terrorist, who also had a practice—
he threatened to kill us, leering around his cigar like Capone,
his voice soaked the telephone in whiskey Easter Sundays,
Your father home? I met him at the door.

Others, I never met. Uncle Gaetano, the cameo-sweet suicide.
An albino on my mother's side, and that mean old lady
who locked herself in when the house caught fire. She died
under the kitchen sink, jewels clenched fast in her fists.

Remember who you come from! You are a Feraca!
Daddy, you stamped us in the coinage of those words
repeated over and over, their final mint the bed
where engines went on growling underneath your head like guard dogs.

3

"U Saraciniello," they called you, my son, sweet saracen,
seeing your skin stained mahogany-dark at birth.
Little do you know you carry in your veins
a strain that might prove darker in a daughter or a son.

This you inherit from me, your mother who married
the son of yet another set of kissing cousins.
You don't get apples from a pear tree, just like my father
always said. *It's in the genes,* woven into the DNA

like fire in the cloth Medea wove that ate the princess' flesh.
There's pestilence breeding in the hope chest kept so long.
Don't touch! the French lace, the monogram, the silk rosette.
Don't trust! the house your grandfather built in Scarsdale.

It all goes home to this: a fist of hovels
gleaming like whitewashed knuckles high on a hill.
There your great-granduncles cut the deck: the kings
dealt with the jacks until the hand played out.

This is your heritage: Eternal Noon, they call it.
Donkey, flies, the clock in the empty piazza,
all of it stopped, sunk in the same stone swoon.
It's time we gave it up. We've kept it in the family

much too long. Listen, at Woodlawn,
where mosses and leaves thicken over the stone steps
and the great gray lions guard the tomb,
Saverio, your great-grandfather, lies inside,

his name graven over the lintel of the family mausoleum,
his bronze bust sprouting green fuzz whenever the rain drips.
Inside his copper coffin, a camellia blooms on his cheek.
Leave it there. Let it feed and deepen. Marry a Hungarian.

Convalescing in the East Sisters' Weavers' House

Shakertown, Kentucky

1

It's white that keeps me straight.
It's white that flutes the linen drape.
It's white that rustles through the window, starched and crisp.
White, with its needleful of sleep.

I'm just this side of nothingness.
I'd be afraid of vanishing,
stepping off
the thin white line
I walk three times a day, afraid the moon
might haul me by the hair
were it not for the white eye of the Eldress, over all.

It's white that keeps me narrow in my bed.
It irons me out flat.
I'm grateful for its weight.

Snow outside.
Death flinging out its endless bolt of cloth.
That must be God out there, driving the hearse behind the glass.
That must be life, standing a little to the side
like a distant cousin at the wake.

I'm in the dead eye of the storm.
Blindness starts the poem.
I cannot lift my body from the page.

2

Muslin boils up at the window, a white broth.

Light sinking from the page
bolts back again, flashing its sword.

Downstairs, a door bangs shut.

A sudden gust, words splattering the ceiling
swarm across the walls.
And now, the light obscured.
I wait.

It is beginning spring.
I'm in a corner of the house, facing north.
Heaving at my feet, a grey tide, while in the east
the sun shakes loose a fringe of buds
that dances sugar-maple red against the blue.
Branches scourge and clash.
Force contends with force.

> *Do I dare believe in you, my life?*
> *my red thread*
> *spun*
> *from the belly's dark,*
> *my daisy stitch on the white edge*
>   *of nothing*

> *Do I dare believe in you, my love?*
> *my rope ladder*
> *dropped*
> *out of the attic dark?*

3

At the base of a trunk
a tingling begins
sap starts its rise along the spine.

Snowflakes swirl, the room filling like a bellows
empties, fills, the mind reels out
reels in

> *When will I take you up, my life?*
> *When, oh little brother,*
> *will I carry you across to the other side?*

I passed you on a sideroad once, driving south from Rome.
Your young arms filled with the new broomcorn
you held out that bright bouquet, yellow as the sun.
I recognized you then.
I almost ran you down.

When the mountains rose along the valley farther south
looming like great-aunts at my birth
I was afraid. I saw their hair
hung down between their thighs like Spanish moss.
I shuddered at the thought of crawling through.

I dreamed of hooks, of holding on.
I built of my heart an underground well
and there I lived inside
crouched for years at the end of a rope.

4

Who is that rapping at the glass?
Who comes to greet me?
What nurse? What angel reaching?

My arms lift over my head a clean gown.
Syllables break like birds from my mouth.
I tug the birth from my thighs with my own hands.
I cut the cord. I wash it clean.
I take up my song.

What do my eyes love?
What has my body embraced?
The head of the child it would have crushed.

The past is done, that bridal train that dragged me down,
I've sloughed it off, a dead skin.
Hands, I forgive your sins,
your grope and fumble;
feet, your stumbling, your clumsy fall through time;
thighs, your yearning, that open beak
I can never fill.
Marry me to the earth, the air.

My body lightens like the snow.
Tenderness washes over me in waves, light blue.
It's so new, this feeling, I hardly recognize it.
It's like the guest who shows up at the wedding uninvited.

This is my own darkness I am making peace with.
I can sit beside her now.
I can listen to her lunatic laughter,
her hands fluttering like doves over her lap.
We are sister travelers waiting for the bus south.

When the bell rings, I help gather up your cardboard boxes.
We are standing in line, waiting to be checked.
A voice announces our departure:

> *Mt. Sterling*
> *Firestone*
> *Slade*
> *Quicksand*
> *Lost Creek*
> *Hazard*
> *Viper*
> *Blue Diamond*
> *Kingdom Come State Park*
> *and points south*
>> *This coach now ready for boarding through the West Gate.*

I am looking for you. I find you in the next seat.
Your shoulder is against mine.
It will be a long trip.
The engines rev as the voice
comes over the intercom for the last time:

> *Ladies and Gentlemen, may I have your attention . . .*